EPIC FAILS

NOT-SO-GREAT
PRESIDENTS:
COMMANDERS IN CHIEF

ERIK SLADER AND BEN THOMPSON

ILLUSTRATIONS BY TIM FOLEY

Roaring Brook Press

New York

To our great country and the
ideals on which it was founded

Text copyright © 2019 by Erik Slader and Ben Thompson
Published by Roaring Brook Press
Roaring Brook Press is a division of Holtzbrinck Publishing Holdings
Limited Partnership
175 Fifth Avenue, New York, NY 10010
mackids.com

Library of Congress Cataloging-in-Publication Data

Names: Slader, Erik, author. | Thompson, Ben, 1980– author. | Foley,
  Tim, 1962– illustrator.
Title: Not-so-great presidents : Commanders in Chief / Erik Slader and
  Ben Thompson ; illustrated by Tim Foley.
Description: First edition. | New York : Roaring Brook Press, 2019. |
  Series: Epic fails | Includes bibliographical references and index. |
  Audience: Grades 4 to 6. | Audience: Ages 8–12.
Identifiers: LCCN 2018020988 (print) | ISBN 9781250150608 (hardcover :
  alk. paper) | ISBN 9781250150592 (pbk. : alk. paper)
Subjects: LCSH: Presidents—United States—Miscellanea—Juvenile
  literature.
Classification: LCC E176.8 .S58 2019 (print) | DDC 973.09/9—dc23
LC record available at https://lccn.loc.gov/2018020988

Our books may be purchased in bulk for promotional, educational, or
business use. Please contact your local bookseller or the Macmillan
Corporate and Premium Sales Department at (800) 221-7945 ext. 5442
or by email at MacmillanSpecialMarkets@macmillan.com.

First edition, January 2019
Book design by Monique Sterling
Printed in the United States of America by LSC Communications,
Harrisonburg, Virginia

Hardcover: 10 9 8 7 6 5 4 3 2 1
Paperback: 10 9 8 7 6 5 4 3 2 1

EPIC FAILS

NOT-SO-GREAT
PRESIDENTS:
COMMANDERS IN CHIEF

"My great concern is not whether you have failed, but whether you are content with your failure."

—Abraham Lincoln

CONTENTS

INTRODUCTION
"Who Is the President Anyway?"

Since the first president took office in 1789, forty-four men have served as the highest-ranking politician in the United States. Each has wielded executive power over one of the foremost countries in the world, serving not only as political leader but also as commander in chief of all American military forces. Each of these men, from George Washington to Donald Trump, has a unique story, unique accomplishments, and unique . . . well . . . failures.

Oh, and since we're talking about failures, even though Trump is known officially as the forty-fifth president of the United States, he's actually the forty-fourth guy to hold the title—because one president (Grover Cleveland) actually had two nonconsecutive terms, and he messed up the count for everyone.

Unlike the Roman emperors or the Russian tsars of long ago, the president of the United States does not wield unlimited power to just rule America with an iron fist. The president is, in fact, a democratically elected politician, and no matter how much he might want to try to steamroll his opposition, the president is bound to the Constitution and held accountable by a system of checks and balances that keep him from getting out of control. So, to keep any one branch of government from dominating the country, the federal government is split among three branches: the judicial (Supreme Court), the legislative (Congress), and the executive (president).

Another big difference between the old medieval kings and the president of the United States of America is that the president is chosen by the people, for the people—just like *American Idol* contestants. Maybe voting for guys as if they're on *Dancing with the Stars* isn't the best idea ever, but it beats the way they used to do it, when power just passed from the king to his son until someone got mad, killed the king, and crowned a new one. No, in America there's a presidential election every four years, where American citizens from all fifty states vote for a new president and then immediately start complaining about him.

There are only three requirements to run for the presidency: You must be a "natural born" citizen (meaning born in the United States), you need to have lived in the United States for at least fourteen years, and you need to be at least thirty-five years old. So any American meeting these requirements can technically become president, but it takes a special kind of person to *be* the president . . .

And as you'll read in this book, just because someone *can* be president, and was *elected* to be president, doesn't mean he *should* be president . . . or that he did a particularly great job!

CHAPTER 1
First Presidents

*"We should not look back unless it is to derive
useful lessons from past errors, and for the purpose
of profiting by dearly bought experience."*

—George Washington

The year was 1776, and the bloody fighting
of the American Revolution was in full swing.
American colonists had openly challenged the
authority of King George III of England, and the
first shots of the conflict rang out over Boston
Harbor and echoed across the Atlantic. While
many brave and poorly equipped American pa-
triots stood their ground against the might of

the British Empire, the members of the Second Continental Congress were frantically scrambling to try to figure out what the heck to do next.

You see, what had started as a slightly rowdy antitax demonstration of protesters cosplaying as Native Americans (the Boston Tea Party) now escalated into a shooting match between the largest military the world had ever seen and a ragtag group of untrained militiamen that was low on gunpowder. If this revolution was going to be a real war for independence, America was going to need a powerful, talented, and effective leader to take command and lead the country to freedom.

On July 4, 1776, members from all thirteen colonies had finally come to an agreement. It was a hot Thursday afternoon at the Pennsylvania State House in Philadelphia. And on that day, the members of the Continental Congress signed

Benjamin Franklin, John Adams, and Thomas Jefferson working hard on writing the Declaration of Independence

their names to the Declaration of Independence, which decreed America's separation from England. The fifty-six delegates who signed the document declaring their independence from Great Britain knew that if they lost the war, they would all be dead men walking—betraying the king of England was a crime punishable by death. Today we know these men as the Founding Fathers, but at the time, they were just rebels-with-a-cause in funny-looking wigs. They were labeled traitors to the Crown.

Founding Father and future president George Washington was not present at this historic signing, mostly because he was too busy getting shot at by redcoats on the battlefield. He ended up being the leader America was looking for, even though, for a famous war hero, General George Washington actually lost a lot of battles. Like, a ton. In fact, Washington lost way more battles than he won.

Contrary to urban legend, George Washington didn't have wooden dentures and never chopped down a cherry tree (it's all a lie!). What is true, though, is that Washington was born on February 22, 1732, to a super-rich colonial family in Virginia and that he inherited his family's entire fortune, like an eighteenth-century Tony Stark.

Regardless of his impressive losing streak as commander in chief of the Continental Army, George Washington was an inspiring leader who never gave up no matter how many times the British beat up his armies. After Washington endured years of tough battles and miserable combat conditions, his luck finally changed late at night on Christmas 1776, when he and his troops crossed the freezing Delaware River under the cover of darkness and led a successful surprise attack on the British garrison at Trenton, New Jersey. That battle dealt the redcoats one of their worst defeats yet. The American soldiers were still far from winning the war, but Washington gave them the hope they needed to persevere.

The war raged on for seven more years, from the bitter lows of Valley Forge to the climactic

General Washington crossing the Delaware during the Revolutionary War. Fun Fact: Washington was joined by future president James Monroe and Alexander Hamilton.

victory at Yorktown, where Lord Cornwallis surrendered to George Washington. Finally, the American colonies managed to secure their freedom from England with the Treaty of Paris in 1783.

Eager to get their young country on the right track, the Founding Fathers came together in the Philadelphia convention and crafted the Constitution we know so well today, along with the Bill of Rights and the basic structure of the federal government.

The preamble read: "We the People of the United States, in Order to form a more perfect Union, establish Justice, insure domestic Tranquility, provide for the common defence, promote the general Welfare, and secure the Blessings of Liberty to ourselves and our Posterity, do ordain and establish this Constitution for the United States of America."

The US Constitution was ratified in 1788, and the new government began in 1789. The only thing left to do was to elect a leader . . .

Not a King but a President

In 1789, the Electoral College unanimously voted in **George Washington** as the first president of the United States. John Adams, who had the second most votes, became his vice president, while Thomas Jefferson served as Washington's secretary of state. Unlike the presidents that followed, Washington actually operated in New York City rather than the current capital. (Washington, DC, hadn't even been built yet!) From the start, he was adamant about having a neutral foreign policy and not getting involved in the business of other countries, which is pretty funny considering how many of his successors have ignored his advice over the years.

Most of Washington's presidency was spent trying to maintain the peace, building a country, and establishing precedents for future presidents. When the Whiskey Rebellion rose up in Pennsylvania, protesting a new tax meant to pay for the debts incurred during the Revolutionary War, Washington personally led the military in to quell the insurgency. Luckily, the protesters disbanded before things got ugly, but to this day it remains the only time in American history when the sitting president led an army in the field.

By far the most impressive thing about Washington, though, is that instead of using the presidency to rule as a king-for-life, the man turned over the keys after his two terms were up. Washington thought it was important to set an example by leaving after eight years—America had just fought a war to overthrow a king, and he didn't want to simply replace one monarch with another. After leaving the presidency behind, he retired to his farm at Mount Vernon, where he focused on his real passion: brewing moonshine (no joke)!

Dueling Presidents

In 1797, **John Adams** became our second president. Unlike Washington, who was loved by pretty much everyone, Adams wasn't as likable of a dude—he faced constant opposition from all angles, from his own vice president, Thomas Jefferson, to his own party, the Federalists.

After a contentious first term, the election of 1800 ended up being one of the wackiest in American history. When fellow Founding Father Thomas Jefferson threw his hat into the ring to oppose Adams, the president took it personally. The candidates were on opposing sides of a schism between the American people: Jefferson was a Democratic-Republican who sided with rural Americans, while Federalists, like Adams, were strong advocates of the constitutional authority of the federal government. Adams versus Jefferson was the no-holds-barred, winner-take-all match of the century!

Sometimes during elections, campaigns can get a little heated, and instead of focusing on the issues at hand, politicians start attacking their opponent—explaining why people shouldn't vote for the other guy, instead of why people should vote *for* them. This is called mudslinging, and it's nothing new. In fact, John Adams and Thomas Jefferson were pioneers of this form of campaigning.

These two Founding Fathers didn't just throw shade at each other, they went above and beyond in trying to out-insult the other. Jefferson first called Adams weak, then Adams retorted by calling Jefferson "a mean-spirited, low-lived fellow." It was like a kindergarten playground face-off between scholars.

Jefferson, claiming to be above such low tactics, instead hired James Callender to do his dirty work. Callender was so effective that he convinced voters that Adams wanted to start a war with France, despite that almost certainly being fake news. Callender was later charged with slander, and Jefferson washed his hands of the whole affair.

In response to the deluge of insults, Adams's campaign ramped up the anti-Jeffersonian rhetoric and claimed that if Jefferson won the election, murder and robbery would be openly taught and practiced, the ground would be soaked with blood, and America would become a nation of criminals. As it turns out, Thomas Jefferson did win the election, and none of Adams's predictions came true.

Thomas Jefferson, famed author of the Declaration of Independence, served two terms as America's third president, from 1801 to 1809. President Jefferson was a champion of education, science, and the pursuit of knowledge. He even sent some of his personal collection—6,487 books!—to the Library of Congress. Dude loved to read, I guess.

During his time in office, Jefferson cut the country's debt in half, unleashed the US Navy on pirates, and was a champion of both religious freedom and the separation of church and state. In 1803, he also carried out the Louisiana Purchase for super cheap from a guy named Napoleon (perhaps you've heard of him?), approximately 828,000 square miles of territory for $15 million! The Louisiana territory would later make up all or part of fifteen states! This was a big deal, because if it wasn't for Jefferson swooping in on this deal, most of North America today would probably belong to France.

In their later years, after decades of heated debate and outright hatred on opposite ends of the political spectrum, Thomas Jefferson and John Adams began writing each other and became close friends, much like Batman and Superman after they stopped punching each other long enough to realize they were on the same side after all. The dynamic duo stayed in touch as the closest of pen pals regardless of their opposing viewpoints.

Both Adams and Jefferson, lifelong frenemies, died on the same day—July 4, 1826—the fiftieth anniversary of the signing of the Declaration of Independence.

CHAPTER 2
Dead Presidents

"The truth will set you free, but first it will make you miserable."

—James A. Garfield

Ever since George Washington set the standard and left office after his second term, thirteen presidents have followed his example by leaving after two terms. The only president to serve more than that was Franklin Delano Roosevelt, who served three terms and was even elected to a fourth, but he passed away soon after. And then there's guys like William Henry Harrison . . .

Whig Presidents

William Henry Harrison first gained national recognition as a war hero in 1811 during the Battle of Tippecanoe in the Indiana Territory. Governor Harrison led an army of one thousand men to take on Tecumseh's rebellion—a Native American tribe (the Shawnee) who were sick and tired of American immigrants moving in and taking all their land. During his campaign to disperse Tecumseh's encampment, as many as seven hundred Shawnee warriors ambushed Harrison's troops! Despite not having the home-field advantage, Harrison and his men held their ground against wave after wave of attack, managing to win the battle. His military success branded him a war hero in the eyes of many Americans, who admired Harrison for protecting lands they felt were rightfully theirs. Years later, during the 1840 presidential election, William Henry Harrison ran as the Whig Party

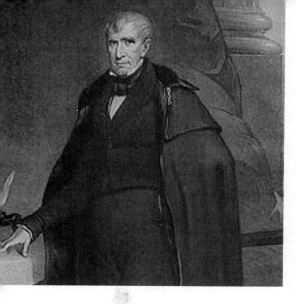

William Henry Harrison, ninth president of the United States, but not for long...

candidate with John Tyler as his running mate. Together the two used the slogan "Tippecanoe and Tyler too!"

Today, the main two political parties are Democrats and Republicans, but before that, we had Democratic-Republicans, Federalists, and Whigs. In modern politics, Democrats tend to be liberal and progressive, while Republicans lean more toward the conservative and traditionalist point of view (even though they started out as the opposite—Republicans used to be liberal, and Democrats used to be conservative). The Whig Party of Harrison and Tyler was a nationalistic movement that opposed the Democratic-Republicans.

Harrison won the election in a landslide, beating out President **Martin Van Buren,** making William Henry Harrison the ninth president of the United States. On March 4, 1841, President Harrison gave the longest inauguration speech ever . . . in the middle of a blizzard—without his coat! Exactly one month later, on April 4, 1841, Harrison died of pneumonia and enteric fever.

Harrison was the first president to die in office, so it was kind of a shock when everyone realized that his vice president, **John Tyler**, was now the guy in charge. After all, "Tippecanoe and Tyler too," while catchy, doesn't exactly make Tyler out to be much more than a tacked-on accessory. The Whig Party had added Tyler (a former Jacksonian Democrat) to the ticket only to appease the pro-slavery voters in the South. Soon after Tyler became president, Harrison's entire cabinet save one resigned!

But Tyler was a notoriously unpopular president—he vetoed nearly everything that came across his desk, annexed Texas as a slave-owning state, and got disowned by his own political party! During his last days in office, Tyler decided to go out with a bang. He sent out about two thousand invitations to a massive party at the White House and over three thousand people showed up. Several barrels of wine and eight dozen bottles of champagne later, the White house was wrecked, and Tyler peaced-out, saying, "They cannot say now that I'm a president without a party."

William Henry Harrison wasn't the only president to die unexpectedly in office, either. In 1850, our twelfth president, **Zachary Taylor**, also died under very unusual circumstances only one year into his term. On July 4, 1850, President Taylor was attending a ceremony at the construction of the Washington Monument on a particularly hot day—where he reportedly ate "copious amounts" of cherries and then practically downed gallons of cold milk and lemonade.

After Taylor stuffed his face, his stomach started to hurt. (Unfortunately, Pepto-Bismol wasn't created until 1901.) Five days later, Taylor officially died of cholera . . . (and eating way too many cherries!) Leaving **Millard Fillmore** to fill his shoes.

The President, Not the Cat

Perhaps one of the most unfortunate and completely avoidable tragedies in the history of American presidents was the death of America's twentieth president, **James A. Garfield**. If there's one thing that defines President Garfield, it was that he was notoriously unlucky. He was so clumsy, in fact, that once during a six-week stint on a boat, he fell overboard a total of fourteen times! And then there's the assassination, though that one had a little less to do with Garfield's being clumsy . . . On July 2, 1881, he was shot at a train station by Charles J. Guiteau, once in the back and once in the arm. Guiteau was convinced that *he* was the sole reason Garfield had been elected president and felt that he deserved to be chosen as the ambassador to France in return—despite never having been to France, not being able to speak French, and, oh yeah, not having ever spoken to President Garfield before.

James A. Garfield, twentieth president of the United States

But here's the really unfortunate thing: Garfield probably would've survived the shooting if it wasn't for the careless surgeons who accidentally tore open his liver and infected the wound in an attempt to remove the bullet . . .

Still, before President Garfield's four-year term was tragically cut to six months, he managed to improve education, reform foreign policy, and fight corruption in . . . the Post Office (?!), where, it turns out, Garfield helped to root out a conspiracy of profiteering rings that stole millions of dollars.

CHAPTER 3
Eccentric Presidents

*"Washington, DC, is twelve square miles
bordered by reality."*

—Andrew Johnson

The office of the president has been known
to attract a certain type of person. There's
certainly a level of ego, ambition, and fortitude
one requires to step into the spotlight—knowing
that you will forever be remembered, but that
you'll also become a very visible target for those
who disagree with you. Ideally, that drive and
courage are also coupled with humility and

respect—knowing that it's an honor to serve one's country at the highest level. It takes an exceptional person to be the leader of the Free World, and sometimes that person is . . . *unique* in more ways than one.

John Quincy Adams (the son of a former president, John Adams) was the first president to denounce slavery, reduced the national debt from $16 million to $5 million, and spoke fluent French, Italian, Russian, German, and Latin! (English, too.) Oh, and while he was secretary of state, he negotiated the purchase of Florida from Spain, so you can also thank him for that, I suppose. He was also a little . . . um . . . unorthodox.

John Quincy Adams was a very eccentric guy, even for nineteenth-century presidents. For starters, he enjoyed taking a long early-morning swim in the Potomac River—*in the nude*! If that's not weird enough for you, John Quincy Adams also once approved an expedition to the center of the Earth in search of . . . mole people?! The voyage was scrapped, however, once Andrew Jackson took office—but not because a mission to the Earth's core was something that belonged in a cheesy 1950s science-fiction movie, but rather because some say Jackson believed the Earth was flat!

After his presidency, Adams (Jr.) was elected to Congress and served as an outspoken abolitionist. In 1841, at seventy-three years young, Adams took up the *Amistad* case, successfully defending the Africans who'd been wrongly and illegally enslaved and tortured, making waves that would later shake the nation to its core. John

Quincy Adams was so dedicated to serving his country that he collapsed midspeech on the floor of the House of Representatives at the age of eighty and died of a stroke.

Wealthy and Wild

Andrew Jackson was a self-made man and saw himself as a champion of the common folk . . . even though he was one of the richest men elected to office, ever. He became the seventh

General Andrew Jackson at the Battle of New Orleans. This painting is considered to be an extremely inaccurate depiction.

president of the United States, after fighting the British during the War of 1812, where he won a significant victory during the Battle of New Orleans . . . after the war was officially over (womp womp).

Jackson was born in South Carolina, and as a young boy he and his brother fought the British during the American Revolution. Unfortunately, Jackson was captured and beaten up by the Brits, left half deaf with a scar across his face. At sixteen, when the war was over, he found himself an orphan. Despite the miserable hand he'd been dealt, Jackson grabbed onto the American dream and rose from poverty to prominence. He eventually became a frontier lawyer and went West, beyond civilization, to claim the untamed land west of Tennessee.

Andrew Jackson, also known as "Old Hickory," became an honorary general and a ruthless Indian hunter. As a member of the House of Representatives, he was known for his violent temper, and he would eventually become one of the the richest US presidents to hold office—a fortune he made by conquering land from the Native Americans and then selling it for a profit.

Now it's worth mentioning that Andrew Jackson (of Jacksonville fame) was a scary man. His face is plastered across the $20 bill, and he sorta looks like Dracula. He was notorious for fighting in more than a hundred duels throughout his life—including one where he still managed to kill his opponent moments after taking a bullet to the chest! Later in his life, he used to joke that he'd been shot so many times that when he moved around his body would rattle like a bag of marbles (ew).

As president, Jackson may have lowered the national debt and improved trade with Europe, but he also made a number of grievous missteps: He divided the country by destroying the National Bank for personal reasons. He also had a gambling problem, anger-management issues, and complete contempt for the judicial system. During the Nullification Crisis, South Carolina threatened to secede because of enormously high import tariffs, which they deemed unconstitutional. In response to the South

The Cherokee during the Trail of Tears—one of the darkest moments in American history

Carolina Legislature, Jackson sent troops to shut them up.

And then there's the infamous Indian Removal Act—his plan to "peacefully" relocate the Native Americans west so America could steal their land. It was a decision that passed Congress by thirteen votes in 1830. As you are probably aware, this event is known today as the Trail of Tears and is perhaps one of the greatest trage-dies in American history—forcing sixteen thou-sand Cherokees (including women and children) to travel 2,200 miles on foot (many in chains) to a land they'd never seen before. The march ended up killing at least four thousand noncombatants and nearly annihilating an entire culture.

The Rough Rider

Teddy Roosevelt is both one of our greatest presidents and one of the most intriguing historical figures to ever live. This guy was a soldier, author, cowboy, father, farmer, sheriff, police commissioner, Harvard graduate, boxer, football enthusiast, mountain climber, big-game hunter, taxidermist, nature conservationist, survivalist, governor, working-class hero, trust buster, Nobel Peace Prize recipient, and president! (Seriously, try to top that résumé!) When a British writer visited the White House in 1903, he came away saying, "Roosevelt is not an American, you know. He is America."

Roosevelt wrote more than thirty-five books

Theodore Roosevelt, twenty-sixth president of the United States

in his lifetime, starting with *The Naval War of 1812* at twenty-three. He once climbed the fifteen-thousand-foot peak of the Matterhorn in the Swiss Alps (during his honeymoon). TR also had a penchant for skinny-dipping in the Potomac River (what is it with all these naked presidents, anyway?), was blinded in his left eye after a boxing injury, and was both a big-game hunter and a nature conservationist who deeply cared about preserving the environment.

In 1897, President William McKinley chose Roosevelt to be the assistant secretary of the US Navy. The following year, in 1898, the Spanish-American War broke out. Without missing a beat, Roosevelt dropped what he was doing, quit his secretary job, and assembled an elite squad of ridiculously tough cavalrymen known as the Rough Riders.

The Rough Riders were the first volunteer cavalry regiment in US history. Under Colonel

Roosevelt, the Rough Riders faced off against Spanish forces in Cuba. Roosevelt and his cavalry led the iconic uphill charge during the Battle of San Juan Hill. TR returned home a hero. He was elected vice president to William McKinley, which—after the assassination of McKinley—led to his becoming the nation's youngest president at just forty-two years old.

Roosevelt accomplished more as president than most during his two terms. He set aside 150 million acres of forest to preserve, roughly doubling the number of national parks. He took on corruption in both government and big business. He signed the Pure Food and Drug Act, established the Department of Commerce and Labor, and became a working-class hero with his expert handling of the 1902 Anthracite Coal Strike in Pennsylvania.

It's also worth noting that the teddy bear itself is actually named after Teddy Roosevelt, because of a story from a hunting trip in which Roosevelt took mercy on a bear that had been tied up just for him to shoot. He thought it was unsportsmanlike. Well, somehow this story got around and became a political cartoon that inspired a candy shop owner in Brooklyn to name his stuffed animal in the president's honor.

One of his biggest accomplishments was the creation of the Panama Canal. The Panama Canal was a massive undertaking: a forty-eight-mile-long waterway that cuts through Panama, connecting the Pacific Ocean to the Atlantic—a huge shortcut for international shipping. The canal project was first started in 1881 by the French, but they gave up on it because of numerous problems, so, in 1904, the United States swept in and took up the challenge.

In one of America's not-so-proudest moments, President Roosevelt used his military power to help overthrow Colombian control of the region and installed a new government. Ultimately, the Panama Canal project went way over budget, costing roughly $375 million, but it was finally completed in 1914. Roosevelt stated, "I took the isthmus, started the canal and then left Congress not to debate the canal, but to debate me."

Many of the countries in Central America and the Caribbean started to get fed up with getting a raw deal and began protesting against their treatment at the hands of "Big Banana." To protect its commercial interests in the tropical fruit trade, the United States sent in the Marines to put a stop to the labor movements by any means necessary. During Roosevelt's administration, police action and military occupations were conducted in Cuba, Panama, the Dominican Republic, and Honduras.

In 1908, TR decided not to seek a third term and chose William Howard Taft to continue his legacy. Roosevelt spent the next few years traveling around the world and hunting lions, rhinos, and elephants on an African safari. In 1910, he became the first president to ride in an airplane— one of the Wright Brothers' early models!

Later on, at fifty-eight years old, during World War I, Roosevelt was ready to ship out and fight alongside American soldiers, but he was advised

against it (Roosevelt's son Quentin did fight and die in that war. His other son, Teddy Jr., would go on to be the highest-ranking officer on Utah Beach during the D-Day invasion of World War II). That's just how tough this guy was. Roosevelt was far from perfect, but there's no doubt he lived life to the fullest and gave 110 percent to everything he put his mind to.

CHAPTER 4
Civil War Presidents

"My failures have been errors of judgment, not of intent."

—Ulysses S. Grant

The Civil War was one of America's darkest hours. This war literally turned brother against brother and nearly tore the country apart. Almost a hundred years since the nation was forged in the crucible of the American Revolution, the United States had gone from thirteen colonies to thirty-four states and counting. In that time, there were a lot of opposing viewpoints on our country's destiny, and it all boiled over in 1861 into America's bloodiest conflict.

When Jefferson first wrote that "all men are created equal," the only people that it seemed to apply to were rich, landowning white men. It was a sentiment that was particularly untrue for millions of African slaves who had been brought to America against their will and forced to work the fields with no rights, no pay, and no control over their own destiny. The Civil War (not to be confused with that time Iron Man and Captain America got into a fight) was about to change all that. While African American slaves toiled on plantations in the South, a small, progressive movement started to gain momentum in the North: the abolitionists.

In the Northern states, antislavery sentiment had finally caught on with the emergence of Free States (states that had declared slavery illegal), while the entire economy of the Southern states was based on slave labor. As Kansas officially joined the Union, the debate over whether it should be a Free State or a slave state threatened to tip the delicate balance and throw the country into further unrest. So in 1861, by the time Kansas was officially admitted as a Free State, six Southern states had already seceded from the Union and formed the Confederate States of America under "President" Jefferson Davis (because the Confederacy was a different country from the United States, Davis is *never* on any list of American presidents. If you put his name down on a quiz, you'll get zero credit, every time).

In response, President Abraham Lincoln declared war against the insurrection in order to preserve the Union. And so thousands of men in super-uncomfortable wool uniforms, armed with muskets and bayonets, marched toward their death in support of their cause . . .

The Road to Civil War

Although **Abraham Lincoln** was president at the time, the conflict had been building for a while. So who really caused the Civil War?

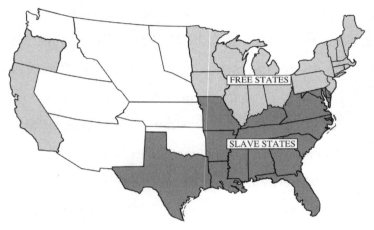

The answer is long and complicated, but several presidents are definitely to blame: John Tyler, James K. Polk, Millard Fillmore, Franklin Pierce, and James Buchanan. It's also worth noting that at the time of Lincoln's historic Emancipation Proclamation, thirteen former or future presidents bought, sold, or owned slaves at one time or another: Washington, Jefferson, Madison, Monroe, Jackson, Van Buren, Harrison, Tyler, Polk, Taylor, Buchanan, Johnson, and even Ulysses S. Grant, the Union general who fought against the Confederacy!

John Tyler annexed Texas as a slave state and even joined up with the Confederacy years later. James K. Polk defended slavery as a right of the Southern states. Millard Fillmore signed the Fugitive Slave Act—which basically made it legal to arrest freed slaves in nonslave states.

Franklin Pierce tried appeasing the Southern states by supporting the Kansas-Nebraska Act, which would repeal the Missouri Compromise— allowing slave states in the North, which furthered the schism over the abolitionist movement. And then James Buchanan came along and basically let the country fall apart . . .

During his tenure as president, Buchanan supported Chief Justice Roger B. Taney in his

James Buchanan, post-presidency

decision concerning the Dred Scott case—
which stated that the federal government had no
right to regulate slavery and that African Americans could not be American citizens. It has since
been criticized as the single worst Supreme
Court decision in the history of the United States
and is cited by many historians as the catalyst
for the Civil War. Furthermore, the "Bleeding

Kansas" crisis, the Utah War, and the Panic of 1857 all happened under Buchanan's watch . . . We're not going to get into too much detail about any of those things here, but they're all just about as bad as they sound.

The Grand Wrestler

After Lincoln's election in 1860, seven states seceded from the Union before his inauguration: South Carolina, Mississippi, Florida, Alabama, Georgia, Louisiana, and Texas! James Buchanan did nothing. Nothing at all . . . and Abraham Lincoln inherited a fractured country on the brink.

"Honest Abe," "the Rail-Splitter," "The Great Emancipator"—Abraham Lincoln was many things to many people, and he still is today. Lincoln is probably the most iconic president in American history, and he is without a doubt one of the most quotable icons in human history, but he was also a far more complex individual than the memorials and shrines would have you believe. That said, most Americans today would probably agree that Lincoln was one of the best examples of what it is to be a great president.

Abe Lincoln was born in a log cabin in Kentucky on February 12, 1809. He grew up on the frontier in Indiana, chopping firewood and helping out with chores on the family farm. While Lincoln didn't mind the physical labor, he often would rather spend his time reading or writing. Lincoln's life was plagued by tragedy from early on. His mother died when he was only nine years old, and years later, his girlfriend, Ann Rutledge, died unexpectedly in 1835. Despite his hardships, Abe was never the type to call it quits.

At six feet four, Lincoln was a towering figure even by today's standards. Lincoln wasn't just huge, either; he was also super-ripped from decades of wielding an ax and wrestling. Yes, wrestling.

Funny thing is, before becoming president (except for being tough as nails), Lincoln failed at basically everything else. He lost at least eight elections and two jobs, and inherited massive debt from a failed business venture. Fortunately, he never once gave up.

In 1836, Lincoln became a self-taught lawyer and made a name for himself with the Kansas-Nebraska Act. As a Whig Party leader, he was elected to the Illinois House of Representatives and later the US House of Representatives. It was there that he made his stance against slavery known, as a moral issue rather than a legal one, leading up to his famous statement: "a house divided against itself cannot stand," meaning

Abraham Lincoln giving his historic Gettysburg Address

that America could not survive as half-slave-owning and half-free—it needed to stand together for freedom. This abolitionist message propelled Lincoln to become the voice of the newly formed Republican Party, eventually landing him the presidency.

After Buchanan's disastrous presidency, Lincoln inherited a White House in ruins. Seven states had seceded and formed the Confederacy, and Washington, DC, itself seemed to be crumbling around him, but Abe never lost his cool. After the Confederate army attacked the American base at Fort Sumter, Lincoln's call to arms united the Northern states.

In 1863, at the height of the bloody fighting of the Civil War, President Lincoln gave the Emancipation Proclamation, which declared slavery unlawful, and he spent the last years of his life rallying for the ratification of the Thirteenth Amendment—the constitutional amendment that ended slavery in America.

While Lincoln did a great many positive things during his time in office, he also did a number of . . . not-so-great things, such as instituting martial law and arresting between ten thousand and fifteen thousand American citizens without a trial!

Ultimately, Lincoln's actions mended the fractured nation, mostly, but the cost of the

Civil War was catastrophic on both sides, with over 785,000 dead (by far the bloodiest war in US history). As fate would have it, before Lincoln could begin the healing process with his plans for Reconstruction, he was assassinated at Ford's Theatre by a disgruntled Confederate conspirator named John Wilkes Booth on April 14, 1865—a mere five days after Confederate general Robert E. Lee surrendered to Ulysses S. Grant to all but bring the Civil War to an end. Over a century later, Lincoln's legacy lives on.

Sir Veto

Lincoln spent his presidency fixing the disaster Buchanan had left him, only to have his successor, **Andrew Johnson**, come in and start breaking things all over again. The country was still on shaky ground after the devastating

Andrew Johnson was the first president to be impeached.

repercussions of the Civil War. More than ever before, the United States needed a president it could depend on to do what was best for all Americans. That president was not Andrew Johnson.

Andrew Johnson was virtually the exact opposite of Lincoln. He was a Jacksonian Democrat who was basically on the side of the

Confederates except for the whole breaking-up-the-country thing. The Republicans had nominated him for vice president (for Lincoln's second term) only because they figured he would gain some sympathy from the Southerners to encourage then to work together. It didn't succeed.

Lincoln and Johnson, a reported alcoholic, met again for the first time since the inauguration on April 14, 1865. Later that night, Lincoln was murdered by John Wilkes Booth, and the very next morning Andrew Johnson was sworn in as the president of the United States.

Andrew Johnson may have been on the side of the Union, but it was abundantly clear he did not have the same agenda as Abraham Lincoln. His first order of business? President Johnson pardoned Confederate leaders who swore allegiance to the Union.

Slavery may have been over, but African Americans had a long way to go before obtaining freedom. They may have been technically "free," but they were now third-class citizens, enslaved by a number of social constructs and crippling poverty, with very little mobility. When Congress met in 1865, Reconstruction was well under way. The Reconstruction era was an attempt to bring the country back together after the Civil War, to rebuild the nation and move forward into the future, with freedom for all.

While the institution of slavery was slowly being done away with, a series of "black codes" began to crop up in its place among the Southern states. These unconstitutional laws allowed farmers to keep African Americans as indentured laborers in contracts they could not quit. Laws also were put in place that allowed law enforcement to arrest African Americans for no reason and then rent them out for labor. Unfortunately, Johnson took the side of the wealthy plantation owners. Whenever Congress presented him with progressive bills to support recently freed slaves, Johnson took great pleasure in vetoing them— using his presidential power to strike them down. When the Civil Rights Act of 1866 came to his desk, President Andrew Johnson vetoed it, but Congress, luckily, overrode him.

The Civil Rights Act of 1866 established (for the first time in American history) that *all* American citizens were equally protected by the law and from discrimination. Congress then ratified the Fourteenth Amendment, which forbade any state to deprive one of life, liberty, or property without due process. However, many Southern states continued to refuse to accept former slaves as equals. By opposing equality for African

Americans, Andrew Johnson set in motion a vicious cycle of racial injustice and animosity that is still felt today.

Because of his actions, in 1868, Johnson became the first US president to be impeached. He was tried under eleven articles of impeachment but was acquitted by only one vote!

General Ulysses S. Grant went on to become the eighteenth president of the United States.

The Hammer

When the Civil War began, **Ulysses S. Grant** answered Lincoln's call to arms and enlisted as a Union soldier. He was soon promoted to brigadier general and found himself commanding twenty thousand strong. In 1862, Grant and his men of the Twenty-First Illinois Volunteer Infantry Regiment stormed Fort Henry and Fort Donelson, where he famously said, "No terms except an unconditional and immediate surrender can be accepted."

Born as Hiram Ulysses Grant, in Ohio, he went on to become one of the most famous generals in American history, despite his notorious reputation as an alcoholic. However, his excessive drinking never seemed to affect his performance on the battlefield. Abraham Lincoln even said, "I wish some of you would tell me the brand of whiskey that Grant drinks. I would like to send a barrel of it to my other generals."

Still, even though he once said that the only reason he'd ever get into politics would be to "fix the pothole outside my house," Grant did manage to pull the country together in a way that Johnson had completely failed to. He established the first national park (Yellowstone) and oversaw the ratification of the Fifteenth Amendment. The Fifteenth Amendment prohibits the federal and state governments from denying any man, regardless of race, the right to vote (unfortunately, women didn't count until 1920, with the Nineteenth Amendment).

In 1868, the Republican Party nominated Ulysses S. Grant to be the eighteenth president of the United States. Despite winning the election twice, President

Grant's time in the White House was much less successful than his time on the battlefield. Grant's cabinet was marred by scandals. When Grant saw an uptick in Southern hate crimes toward African Americans by the KKK, he attempted to annex Santo Domingo, the capital of the Dominican Republic, as a colony for freed slaves. (Congress voted against it.) And then there's the Great Sioux War between the US government and the Great Plains Indians over control of the Black Hills—which ended in Native Americans once again being deported from their own land.

CHAPTER 5
Unlucky Presidents

"Blessed are the young, for they shall inherit the national debt."

—Herbert Hoover

There have been many great presidents who were the right man at the right time. The legacies of George Washington, Abraham Lincoln, Teddy Roosevelt, FDR, and JFK live on because they were the right choice for the job at hand. There's no doubt that the times in which presidents serve define them. And then there are the presidents who, through no fault of their own, were thrown into circumstances that were completely out of their control.

James Madison was by no means a bad president, but the White House did kinda burn down on his watch—*seriously*!

At five feet four and only 122 pounds, Madison was small, frail, and epileptic, but that didn't stop him from basically crafting our entire government structure. Madison was busy making a name for himself well before commander in chief-ing. That whole checks-and-balances thing? His idea.

James Madison, Founding Father, author of the Constitution, creator of the Bill of Rights, and fourth president of the United States, was an extremely accomplished man, but nothing could prepare him (and America) for a rematch with Great Britain in the War of 1812. After numerous incidents in which British frigates attacked US ships and stole American sailors, compounded with evidence that the British were supplying guns to Native Americans to combat American settlers, President Madison decided to declare war. The only problem was, the United States was still extremely outmatched against the British Empire.

Although America managed to hold its own, it wasn't exactly a victory, either. The United States decided to take this opportunity to "liberate" Canada in the fight against the Crown, but

Depiction of naval warfare during the War of 1812, the second war between Great Britain and the United States

Canada very politely said no thanks before kicking us to the curb. Meanwhile, the British managed to capture multiple American cities and (like we mentioned before) even burned down the White House!

Painting by Tom Freeman depicting the burning of the White House on August 24, 1814, during the War of 1812

The First Lady, Dolley Madison, helped recover as many priceless paintings and artifacts as she could carry, safeguarding our nation's most valuable national treasures, including one of the only surviving portraits of George Washington! Despite all the setbacks, Madison's resolve pulled the country together during one of its darkest hours and peacefully ended the conflict with the Treaty of Ghent.

The Partiless President

Franklin Pierce was once arrested for running over a lady with his horse—while president! (Similarly, Ulysses S. Grant was also once pulled over for speeding—on his horse—also as president!) Franklin Pierce was elected president because of his moderate stances on a lot of issues, and because he was able to get along with just about everyone. But when he left office, he was *hated* by just about everyone. During his tenure in office, he could best be described as charming, indecisive, and alcoholic.

He also has one of the most tragic back-stories since the Punisher first showed up in Marvel comics. Pierce's life was one of constant tragedy. All three of his children died young—two of them from disease, and then his son Benny was killed in a train wreck in front of his parents not long after the election. Then, just six weeks after the inauguration, his vice president, William R. King, died.

The Union deteriorated around him, and he was abandoned by his own party. As he was leaving the White House, Pierce is quoted as saying, "There's nothing left to do but get drunk." And that's exactly what he did. Pierce returned home in defeat. After his wife passed away, he took up binge drinking as a full-time gig and became a hermit. He died of cirrhosis of the liver because of the insane amounts of alcohol he consumed toward the end of his life.

The irony was that his wife once asked him to

promise not to get involved in politics. This is why (if you ever decide to get married) you should always listen to your spouse. Happy wife = happy life.

President Franklin Pierce was once arrested, as president, for running over a woman with his horse!

The Big Lub

William Howard Taft, who was by far our largest, most rotund president, took office in 1909. At a whopping three hundred–plus pounds,

William Howard Taft, twenty-seventh president of the United States

Mr. Personality himself, Taft was a big guy in every respect. After graduating from Yale (second in his class), he was offered a "chair of Law" at the university, to which he jokingly asked if they could make it a "sofa of Law."

Taft's presidency was . . . mostly forgettable. Not terrible, but not great, either.

President Taft made headway against government and corporate corruption, but he also did a lot of backpedaling in regard to civil rights. President Taft initiated eighty antitrust suits, while adopting policies that discriminated against African Americans, preventing them from getting jobs in government positions. He also had a bad habit of falling asleep during important meetings.

Unfortunately, none of that really matters, though, because William Howard Taft will forever be known as the president who got stuck in the White House bathtub!

According to Ike Hoover's book, *42 Years in the White House*, it allegedly took multiple White House staffers to hoist Taft out of the bath, and some claim they needed butter to slide him out . . . Needless to say, a larger bathtub was soon installed.

Surveyor of Hooverville

The year **Herbert Hoover** became president just so happened to be the year Wall Street crashed and burned. October 24, 1929, known as "Black Thursday," was the day investors nervously began selling off all their shares. Not long after that, nearly five thousand US banks declared bankruptcy. The entire American economy tanked overnight. The Great Depression had begun . . .

No matter what he did, President Hoover would forever take the blame for the economic crisis, despite the fact that the presidents who came before him, Calvin Coolidge and Warren G. Harding, were far more directly responsible. Nine million people had just lost their life savings, and they wanted someone to blame. Hoover was somewhat slow to act, but at least he tried to alleviate the situation. Unfortunately, his plan was to raise everyone's taxes.

As you might expect, that didn't work.

Hoover didn't seem to grasp the severity of the situation when he said, "Nobody is actually starving." Thousands of jobless men, women, and children lived in shantytowns outside cities that soon became known as Hoovervilles, and they dubbed the old newspapers they slept under as Hoover blankets.

CHAPTER 6
Corrupt Presidents

"When the president does it, that means that it is not illegal."

—Richard Nixon

***P**olitical corruption is nothing* new. A century ago, corporate monopolies, rigged elections, and politicians in the pockets of big business were a dime a dozen. From the late eighteen hundreds to the early nineteen hundreds, American industry was booming, but without government regulation, the little guy got steamrolled by the greedy and powerful.

Chester A. Arthur never wanted to be president. Arthur only ever wanted to be vice president, because he wanted the power without responsibility. And then President James A. Garfield was shot in 1881 . . . Suddenly, Arthur had the weight of the world on his shoulders. And then he surprised everyone by going after the very corruption that had gotten him elected in the first place!

Arthur, a Vermont native, became a New York lawyer in 1859. It was after the Civil War, when he did everything in his power to avoid going into combat, that Arthur made connections with several prominent party bosses. These bosses, including the notorious criminal Boss Tweed, were deeply entrenched in the spoils system, a political machine that essentially allowed politicians to buy their way into key positions through the use of bribes and favors. At the time, the New York Custom House (a government office that

Chester A. Arthur, twenty-first president of the United States

deals with imports and exports) was so entrenched in corruption that an elite ring of obscenely wealthy old guys basically ran all of New York City. They were kinda like mobsters before the Mafia was even a thing.

In 1871, Senator Roscoe Conkling, a party boss for the Stalwart Republicans, pulled some strings and got President Ulysses S. Grant to select Chester A. Arthur as the customs collector for the Port of New York. The customs collector was a federal position to oversee import tariffs (taxes on imported goods). As New York's collector, Arthur controlled over a thousand jobs, charged enormous fees on imports, and made at least $50,000 a year! In the eighteen hundreds, that was more like a million. Arthur was living the good life. In return for this prestigious appointment, Arthur handed out government jobs to Senator Conkling's friends, who then donated a portion of their earnings to the party.

Then, in 1878, President **Rutherford B. Hayes** decided to tackle government corruption. While reforming the federal patronage system, Hayes fired Arthur as New York's collector. In response, when Garfield won the 1880 presidential nomination, Senator Conkling worked with the Stalwart Republicans to get one of their own on the ticket: Chester A. Arthur himself.

But when Arthur took over after Garfield's death, no one expected him to turn on the very people who had gotten him elected. In his first presidential address to Congress, Chester A. Arthur made civil service reform his number one goal! (Civil servants are nonelected people employed by the government.) Arthur had a change of heart and immediately started selling out the corrupt party bosses who had helped him win the nomination. In 1883, President Arthur signed the Pendleton Civil Service Reform Act, which made it illegal to promote government officials on anything other than merit and forbade the firing of certain federal positions for politically motivated reasons.

According to a journalist, Alexander McClure, "No man ever entered the presidency so profoundly and widely distrusted as Chester Alan Arthur, and no one ever retired . . . more generally respected, alike by political friend and foe."

Chester A. Arthur may have been one of the most corrupt politicians to ever become president, but he actually used his position to clean up the same corruption that had gotten him elected in the first place.

The Idol of Ohio

In 1896, former Ohio governor **William McKinley** ran for president. McKinley's campaign was funded by a rich senator and industrialist named "Dollar Mark" Hanna, which, of course, indebted McKinley to big business—creating a major conflict of interest. By then, the spoils system (the act of giving government positions to friends and supporters in exchange for help winning an election) may have become a thing of the past, but corruption was alive and well at the dawn of corporate America. McKinley's supporters started a smear campaign against his Democratic opponent, William Jennings Bryan, insisting that Bryan wanted to shift completely from the gold standard to silver, which would vastly change the American economy. It was untrue, but it was good enough to scare voters into voting for McKinley.

As bad as McKinley's corporate-sponsor scandal looked, it was nothing compared with what came next . . . In 1898, American tensions with Spain were at an all-time high when an American battleship, the USS *Maine*, was sunk off the coast of the Spanish colony of Cuba!

The explosion turned out to be an accident, but that didn't stop President McKinley from declaring war on Spain. The Spanish-American War waged for 113 days and is considered one of the most one-sided conflicts in recent history. Not only was the war fought over a pretext, McKinley and his cabinet used the Cuban incident to expand the United States as a global power by becoming an empire. The United States took this opportunity to conquer Cuba, Puerto Rico, Guam, and the Philippines. The Spanish-American War cost the lives of four thousand American soldiers, but that was nothing compared with the lives lost on the opposing side.

The Philippines in particular suffered the most, with over a million casualties, many of which were innocent bystanders. US forces used machine guns and terror tactics against native Filipino guerrilla warriors with spears and bows. The entire occupation (from a war based on a lie) is without a doubt one of the most evil acts ever committed in the name of America.

William Jennings Bryan declared, "We said we are going to bring prosperity and democracy to the Filipinos. But we had better not educate them, because they might learn to read the Declaration of Independence." Mark Twain was also very vocal about how un-American it all was, saying that the American flag should switch out its white stripes for black stripes and its stars for skulls and crossbones.

On September 6, 1901, President McKinley was shot by a deranged anarchist (Leon Czolgosz) while shaking hands with supporters at the inter-national Pan-American Exposition in Buffalo, New York. Immediately after he was shot, his

The last photograph of William McKinley, taken moments before his assassination on September 6, 1901

first concern was for his wife and then for his own assassin. When he was rushed to the hospital, the only surgeon available specialized in women's health and wasn't able to find the bullet. He died eight days later because of a gangrene infection in the bullet wound.

President with Friends in Low Places

To say that **Warren G. Harding**'s term as president was a troubled one would be like saying maybe the Star Wars prequels could have been better. We've had some pretty corrupt politicians in the Oval Office, but few hold a candle to the Harding administration. Chester A. Arthur might've been one of the most corrupt politicians elected as president, but Warren G. Harding's entire cabinet was brimming with corruption.

After World War I, Harding was elected to the presidency with the help of big business and the

Warren G. Harding, twenty-ninth president of the United States

empty promise of a "return to normalcy," a chance for the American people to heal after the war. It was anything but. Sure, he eased restrictions on immigration, fought for civil rights equality, and was involved in numerous foreign treaties (including the Treaty of Versailles), but he also rolled back some of the policies that combated corporate corruption in Washington and gave tax breaks to his wealthy friends.

And then there's the Teapot Dome scandal . . .

In case it's ever a question on *Who Wants to*

Be a Millionaire, the Teapot Dome scandal involved one of the biggest white-collar crimes in American politics. President Harding's secretary of the interior, Albert B. Fall, was paid off to lease out American oil fields to private investors. The Teapot Dome fields in Wyoming were given to Harry F. Sinclair (of Sinclair Oil), while an oil deposit in Elk Hills, California, was given to Fall's buddy, Edward L. Doheny.

Turns out that both Doheny and Sinclair paid Fall over $400,000 (approximately $4.8 million now). Albert B. Fall was found guilty of selling America off to the highest bidder and was thrown into prison, becoming the first former presidential cabinet member to serve jail time for crimes committed while in office.

There's a reason Warren G. Harding is often at the top (bottom?) of the list of worst presidents ever, because he really did suck at his job and might even have been impeached if he hadn't died unexpectedly of a heart attack.

Harding himself once said, "I am not fit for this office and never should have been here."

Tricky Dick

Richard M. Nixon didn't start off as a terrible president, but nowadays he's remembered as one of the most corrupt dudes to ever hold the office! Nixon inherited a country torn apart by war and political unrest, and he moved forward with a plan to bring America together again. When he took office, Nixon actually did a lot of cool stuff—he created the Environmental Protection Agency, oversaw a cooperative US-Soviet space mission (Apollo-Soyuz) in 1972, ended the Vietnam War, signed a treaty with the Soviet Union that took the world one step further away

Richard M. Nixon, thirty-seventh president of the United States

from a nuclear war, negotiated peace between Israel and a number of Arab states, and oversaw the desegregation of schools in the South. In fact, he was so well liked among the American people that he won reelection in 1972 by one of the biggest margins of victory in the history of the Electoral College, when he beat George McGovern 520–17!

Of course, there's also a chance he stole that victory by wiretapping his enemies. And that's what he ultimately went down for.

On June 17, 1972, five men were caught trying to break into the headquarters of the Democratic National Committee in Washington, DC. The headquarters were in an office complex called Watergate, and after they were busted, it turned out that those men were actually there to plant wiretaps in the Democratic Party's campaign offices!

The Watergate story is a really fascinating affair, and a lot of it is centered on two journalists named Bob Woodward and Carl Bernstein, who were working for the *Washington Post* at the time. At first, this wiretapping story wasn't a big deal. But Woodward and Bernstein thought something was weird, and they kept digging. With the help of a secret informant known only as "Deep Throat," the journalists started gathering more and more information, unveiling a bigger and bigger conspiracy . . . one that went all the way to the White House.

First, they found out that the break-in wasn't just a group of random thugs . . . These were operatives who had verifiable ties with the FBI and the CIA! Spying on American citizens is bad enough, but conspiring to tamper with an election was even worse than that. Did Nixon himself know about it? Before long, the Watergate news was the top headline of every paper in America.

Congress put together a special committee to investigate what the heck was going on, but not too long after they started, Nixon fired the special prosecutor in charge of the case! Still, the investigation continued, and it came to light that Richard Nixon had secretly recorded most of the conversations he had in the Oval Office. He was forced to turn over the tapes, which he did, but not before he "accidentally" deleted about eighteen minutes worth of conversations. So . . . yeah.

That wasn't a good look for his being innocent.

The public and Congress turned against Nixon in a hurry, and on August 9, 1974, Richard M. Nixon became the first (and, as of the time of this writing, only) American president to resign his office rather than face impeachment. Nixon was still on the hook to be tried in court (and possibly go to jail!) for illegal wiretapping, but the next president, Gerald Ford, pardoned him so he wouldn't have to go through a trial.

When the smoke cleared, forty-eight of Nixon's staff members were convicted of crimes and put into jail, including Nixon's chief of staff. It was such a huge scandal that nowadays anytime something bad happens in everything from politics to sports, people tag "-gate" onto the end of it to show that it's a big, evil conspiracy.

It's also worth noting that Richard Nixon liked eating cottage cheese with ketchup . . .

which (according to the authors of this book) is grounds enough to have him thrown into jail.

CHAPTER 7
World War Presidents

"A pessimist is one who makes difficulties of his opportunities, and an optimist is one who makes opportunities of his difficulties."

—Harry S. Truman

World Wars I and II were the two most destructive events in human history. During the bloody twentieth century, wars and fighting raged across every continent on earth as men and war machines rained death and destruction everywhere they went. The World Wars reshaped human history and resulted in an unimaginable number of deaths, but in both cases the forces of the United States of America helped bring peace and turn the tides of the conflict. Perhaps even more amazingly, the majority of both of these wars were overseen by just two American presidents!

Woodrow Wilson was born in Virginia in 1856. As a young boy, he had seen firsthand the horror and brutality of war—Wilson's father was the town minister, and the tiny church he oversaw was used as a field hospital during the Civil War, where surgeons and nurses worked tirelessly to save the lives of wounded men. Wilson hated war, and he didn't want anything to do with it . . . which makes it kind of strange that he's the president who got America involved in World War I!

Wilson was the president of Princeton University and then the governor of New Jersey, and he won a wild presidential election in 1912, when he ran against William Howard Taft and Teddy

Roosevelt at the same time. He became the last American president to travel to his inauguration ceremony by horse-drawn carriage, because the world and the technology in it were rapidly changing.

As president, Wilson did some cool stuff and also some not-so-cool stuff. Under his administration, women finally (finally!) got the right to vote, which is awesome, but on the other hand he also passed a law called Prohibition, which made it illegal to buy alcohol, which a lot of people really hated.

However, by far the biggest cloud hanging over the Wilson administration was the horrible violence and destruction going down in Europe. In 1914, the world was at war—Germany, the Ottoman Empire (based in present-day Turkey), the Austro-Hungarian Empire, and eventually Bulgaria, were on one side, and England, France, Russia, and Italy were on the other. Both sides drew lines, dug trenches, and used brand-new technology like airplanes, submarines, and machine guns to decimate one another at a rate that pretty much horrified everyone involved.

Wilson faced a tough call—should America help out or mind its own business?

Well, in 1917, it became impossible to ignore the carnage in Europe any longer. It was in this year that spies intercepted the Zimmerman Telegram, a secret coded message from Germany to Mexico. The deal was, if Mexico invaded America, Germany would help it get back the land it lost in the Mexican-American War! As if that wasn't bad enough, Germany also declared unrestricted submarine warfare, meaning that the German submarine fleet would be free to blast any ships it wanted—including the American ships transporting weapons to England!

Wilson wasn't very happy about this, and in 1917, he went to Congress and asked them to declare a "war to end all wars" in order to "make the world safe for democracy."

At the end of the war, President Wilson saw an opportunity to try to prevent this sort of thing from ever happening again. He proposed a new idea—a League of Nations all working together to try to resolve differences without having to resort to war. If that kind of sounds like the United Nations, that's because that's exactly what he was trying to make!

But, unfortunately, it didn't actually work out in 1918. There was a lot of bad blood across Europe, and the American people really weren't interested in joining any worldwide governments, so talks ultimately broke down pretty quickly. The League of Nations was formed, without America, and the Treaty of Versailles that ended World War I was so brutally harsh on Germany that it caused the country's entire government and economy to collapse a few years later. Wilson got the Nobel Peace Prize for his role in the peace treaty, but it was only a small consolation.

Wilson had a stroke in the fall of 1919 and was essentially in a coma. Wilson's wife, Edith Bolling Galt Wilson, helped with many of his presidential decisions from late 1919 until the new president took over in March 1921. So, while as of the time of this writing we still haven't elected a woman president of the United States, there

First Lady Edith Wilson posing with her husband, President Woodrow Wilson, in 1920

was a woman playing a large role in the job for a year and a half in the early twentieth century.

The Man in Charge

The terrible economic sanctions placed on the German people led to the rise of a man who promised to make his country great once again: Adolf Hitler. Hitler was a loud, power-hungry, charismatic leader who promised to end the economic stress on Germany and build a new *Reich* (empire) that would span all of Europe. His conquest and annexation of other European countries would eventually lead to the beginning of the Second World War.

Meanwhile, in the United States, as the Great Depression saw thirteen million Americans out of work, things were also bleak. There were no jobs, and food was often hard to come by. The American people needed a visionary leader who would not only bring the country out of economic disaster but also (eventually) have to take a stand against Hitler and Nazi Germany as well.

In 1932, they elected **Franklin Delano Roosevelt**.

FDR was a diplomat from New York (and a distant relative of Theodore Roosevelt) who was about as different as you might imagine from a guy who was going to help fight the Nazis. He collected stamps. He became a lawyer. And, for the most part, FDR was a pretty mild-mannered dude . . . a very different bird from Adolf Hitler with his fiery diatribes.

FDR had also caught a crippling disease called polio in 1921, and the disease made it very difficult for him to walk. To appear strong to the American people, FDR would stand and deliver his speeches, but anytime the cameras were turned off, he used a wheelchair to get around.

When FDR came into office, he immediately went to work trying to alleviate the devastation of the Great Depression. He got started on a project he called the New Deal. Basically, his plan was to create ways for the government to better provide for the poorer people in America. He created jobs by ordering the construction of thousands of miles of roads and bridges, putting huge numbers of men to work. He raised taxes on the wealthy and put controls on banks. He created the Social Security program, ensuring that the elderly were taken care of after they could no longer work, and he began the Tennessee Valley Authority, a huge project that brought flood control, electricity, and economic development to a huge part of the Tennessee Valley.

World War II officially began when Hitler invaded Poland in 1939, but once again the American people were undecided on whether to join the fight. America made a lot of money selling tanks and guns to Britain and the USSR, but Roosevelt didn't really want to send soldiers off to die in Europe once again. So, just as it had done in World War I, America stayed silent while

Germany conquered Poland and France, over-ran large parts of the USSR, and launched non-stop air attacks on the British Isles.

That all changed on December 7, 1941, which FDR would later call "a date which will live in infamy." The Imperial Japanese Navy, allies with Germany, launched a surprise air attack at the American naval base in Pearl Harbor, Hawaii, killing 2,403 Americans in the devastating

The Japanese attack on Pearl Harbor on December 7, 1941—"a date which will live in infamy"—FDR

ambush. Many American battleships were damaged or destroyed.

The Japanese thought that with one show of overwhelming power, they could get the United States to cower and cry to their mommas. They didn't think Americans were tough enough for a real fight.

They were wrong.

On the Front

Seven future American presidents fought during the Second World War, between 1941 and 1945.

Ronald Reagan was a super-famous Hollywood actor at this point, and he enlisted immediately in the First Motion Picture Unit, a group of film professionals who made propaganda and training films for the US Army Air Force, including the original movie about the *Memphis Belle*, a famous B-17 bomber.

George H. W. Bush flew Avenger torpedo bombers from the *San Jacinto* in the Pacific. He survived fifty-eight combat missions, was shot down once, and earned three Air Medals and the Distinguished Flying Cross.

Gerald Ford served aboard the light aircraft carrier *Monterey* through many battles in the Pacific. Ford was once almost washed off the deck of the ship during a storm! Richard Nixon was also a sailor, and he was commander of Combat Air Transport operations at Guadalcanal and the Solomon Islands, where he coordinated C-47 transport planes coming into and out of the action. Lyndon Johnson received a Silver Star for his role in a B-26 bomber attack on Japanese installations at New Guinea.

John F. Kennedy was a young lieutenant in the Navy during the war, serving in the Pacific as the commander of a PT-109 patrol boat. While scouting around the Solomon Islands, the PT-109 was ambushed and rammed by a Japanese destroyer ship, which ripped apart the small gunboat. Kennedy and ten of his crew swam to a nearby island and evaded capture for a week before they were finally rescued. JFK received a Navy and Marine Corps Medal for his leadership during the ordeal.

Despite all these heroic deeds during WWII, nobody really comes close to Dwight D. Eisenhower. Eisenhower was the supreme commander of all Allied Forces in Europe—a really tough job in which he had to manage the rampaging egos of a bunch of hotheaded subordinate commanders, get the armies of America, Britain, and France to all work together, and, oh yeah, *plan and execute the Allied invasion of Normandy*. Using his guts, brains, and a heck of a lot of patience, Eisenhower coordinated the D-Day attacks at Normandy, the ground war against Hitler, and personally oversaw the defeat and surrender of Nazi Germany, ending World War II in Europe. So we'd say that's a pretty good job.

Back on the home front, President Roosevelt gave what he called "fireside chats" to the American public to let everyone know what was happening with the war. Not too many people had TVs at this time, so families had to listen to the radio for all their multimedia needs. Clearly, people were down with FDR's radio broadcasts, because he won an unprecedented *four* terms as president. It's something that will never happen

FDR at the mic for one of his famous "fireside chats" broadcasts

again because, in 1951, the Constitution was amended to say that no president can serve more than two terms in office. FDR is (and always will be) the only president who served more than two.

While FDR was a great president in a lot of

ways, he also made some huge mistakes. By far his worst offense was the brutal internment of Japanese Americans in detention camps during the war. Over 100,000 innocent American citizens of Japanese descent were rounded up and put into internment camps against their will. It fueled (and validated) hateful bigotry. These actions tore families apart and cast an entire population of people as undesirable and untrustworthy, resulting in huge economic, social, and cultural losses for Japanese Americans. Not exactly America's proudest moment.

The Closer

Despite leading the country out of the Depression and through the Second World War, Roosevelt wouldn't live to see the final fall of Nazi Germany. He died on April 12, 1945, of a cerebral hemorrhage, and was succeeded by his vice president, **Harry S. Truman**. When Truman took office, the war in Europe was essentially over, but he now had an incredibly difficult decision to make regarding the war in Japan.

American scientists had finally constructed an atomic bomb, and one of Truman's first decisions as president was whether to drop nukes on Japan.

Truman held two plans in his hands: One would see the deaths of hundreds of thousands of innocent civilians. The other would see the deaths of an estimated half a million American soldiers.

On August 6, 1945, the B-29 Superfortress *Enola Gay* dropped the first atomic bomb ever used in warfare over the Japanese city of Hiroshima. More people died in a split second than there were soldiers killed at the Battle of Gettysburg from both Northern and Southern armies combined. Most of those people were civilians.

The mushroom cloud from the atomic bomb "Fat Man" shortly after it was dropped on Nagasaki, Japan

On August 9, it happened again—this time in Nagasaki, Japan.

A week later, the Japanese surrendered. World War II was over, at a terrible cost in human lives.

CHAPTER 8
Cold War Presidents

*"I hate war as only a soldier who has lived
it can, only as one who has seen its brutality,
its futility, its stupidity."*

—Dwight D. Eisenhower

President Harry S. Truman might have ordered the atomic bombs that ended World War II, but no sooner had that conflict ended than another global confrontation began.

Two world wars had taken a pretty serious toll on the rest of the European powers, and from the ashes of the Second World War two great superpowers emerged: the United States of America and the Union of Soviet Socialist Republics—the USSR.

The USSR (also known as the Soviet Union) was a large country, based in Russia, that encompassed many other countries that are independent today. The USSR was a Communist dictatorship, meaning that basically everything it stood for was the complete opposite of American democracy and capitalism.

The Americans and the Soviets didn't like each other, and they didn't trust each other, either. They would spend the years between 1945 and 1991 actively trying to undermine and destroy each other. Because no actual bullets were (officially) fired directly between the Soviets and the Americans, this decades-spanning conflict is known as the Cold War.

The tension began brewing almost immediately after WWII ended, but when the Soviet Union developed nuclear weapons in 1949, it became very clear that any direct battle between the USSR and the United States was going to run the risk of a nuclear holocaust, millions of deaths, and possibly even—no joke—the end of the world.

If one of these countries was going to defeat the other, it would need to find a way to do it without directly invading or opening fire on each other.

One of the main conflict zones of the Cold War was Berlin. After WWII, the Allies and the Soviets split Germany in half, into democratic West Germany and Communist East Germany, but Berlin was well inside the East German border. Part of the deal that ended

the Second World War said that Berlin would also be split into a Communist East and democratic West, but in 1948, the Soviets decided to cut off Allied access to the city and prevent any help or supplies from reaching West Berlin.

Truman responded by sending a massive fleet of cargo planes to provide supplies, food, medicine, and other goods into West Berlin twenty-four hours a day, seven days a week, until the Soviets gave up and decided to reopen the roads. They did, however, get so tired of people fleeing from East Germany to West Berlin that in 1961 they built a huge wall around West Berlin and shot down anyone who tried to flee to the West.

Truman ran for reelection in 1948, and the election was so close (and ran so late) that newspapers had an Epic Fail of their own—the morning after the election of 1948, huge headlines across the country proclaimed DEWEY DEFEATS TRUMAN. Which, of course, isn't what happened. But it does make for a pretty funny picture.

Truman had some problems at home, particularly in the South, where laws known as "Jim Crow Laws" were being passed in several states. These laws stated that black people and white people should go to separate bathrooms and separate schools and basically have nothing to do with each other. This systemic racism became known as segregation, another in a long line of racial problems in the United States,

and Truman has to take a lot of the blame for allowing such a horrible thing to transpire under his watch.

He was also responsible for Executive Order 9835, better known as the "Loyalty Order," which he signed on March 21, 1947. This order gave birth to what was known in America as the "Red Scare"—the perceived fear that Communists and Soviet spies had infiltrated every part of American culture and government and that enemy spies could be anywhere. People started to distrust their neighbors, their friends, and their elected officials. A particularly zealous senator named Joe McCarthy started publicly accusing members of the media, Hollywood, and basically anyone who disagreed with him of being Communists and traitors to America. It was a pretty scary time in the United States— not just because this tactic was designed to make you fear your neighbors but also because you could never be quite sure if you'd say the wrong thing and your neighbors would suddenly think you were a Soviet spy!

Meanwhile, war was beginning to rage across Asia. China had fallen into a civil war of its own, with Communists and Nationalists killing one another in unbelievable numbers all across the country. The Communists, backed by the Soviet Union, eventually routed the Nationalists, sending them into exile on the island of Taiwan.

Truman tried to help the Nationalists in China, but when that failed, he set his sights on defending another region that had come into the crosshairs of the Communists—Korea. In 1950, a revolution in northern Korea, backed by the Communist Chinese, began an invasion of southern Korea in an attempt to conquer it for Communism.

Fighting raged across the Korean Peninsula for years as the United Nations battled North Korea and China in brutal fighting all across the countrvside. Hundreds of thousands of soldiers were killed and wounded, and millions of civilians were killed or displaced from their homes in the bloodiest war since WWII, as the forces of the Communists and Western Allies clashed with tanks, machine guns, and even hand-to-hand combat.

General Ike

Truman gave way to a new president in 1953: **Dwight D. Eisenhower**, the American military hero who had commanded the Allies to victory in the Second World War. Eisenhower, better

Dwight D. Eisenhower, thirty-fourth president of the United States

known by his nickname, "Ike," was commanding troops in Europe when he decided to run for
president. And because he was probably the
most famous guy in America, he won election
pretty easily. Ike stayed tough on the Soviet Union,
but he was also a hard-core military vet who did
not have any interest in seeing more bloodshed

during his lifetime. He negotiated peace in the Korean War almost immediately, with the cease-fire truce dividing Korea into Communist North Korea and democratic South Korea. The borders drawn in 1953 are the same borders between those countries today. North and South Korea never actually declared peace between their countries, meaning that they are technically still at war as of 2018!

At home, Ike built the interstate highway system, so anytime you're driving around on I-95 or I-5 or I-10, you're using a road system set up during the Eisenhower administration. He worked hard to try to desegregate schools in the South, even sending National Guard troops to enforce desegregation at some schools in Alabama and Arkansas—a bold tactic that made some very influential and important first steps toward diversity rights for all Americans. Ike also created NASA in 1958, one year after the Soviets launched Sputnik into orbit, the world's first satellite.

He Was Called Jack by His Friends

After Ike came **John F. Kennedy**, who, when he was elected, was the second-youngest president in American history. JFK was an Irish Catholic, a WWII war hero, and a Pulitzer Prize–winning author, but a lot of people credit his win on his performance in the first American presidential debate ever aired on TV. Kennedy was handsome, charming, and well-spoken, but his opponent (future President Richard Nixon) was sweating like crazy!

JFK continued the American policy of standing up to the Communists in the Cold War, but during his administration, the stakes went up. Like, *way up*.

JFK was a loving father, gave most of his money to charity, and is considered one of the most inspiring leaders of the twentieth century. In his all-too-brief tenure, Kennedy worked to end segregation and helped ignite America's space

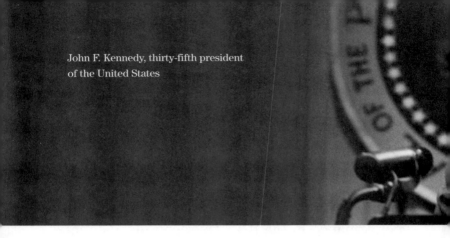

program. Unfortunately, soon after being elected, Kennedy found himself thrown into the deep end of one of the most intense political crises of our time: the Cuban Missile Crisis.

In 1959, a Communist revolution in Cuba, led by Fidel Castro and Che Guevara, overthrew the government and suddenly installed a Soviet-backed dictatorship on an island just ninety miles from Florida.

Eventually, Kennedy responded to the Cuban Revolution by giving CIA assistance to a group of anti-Communist Cuban guerrillas who were

planning to invade Communist Cuba, overthrow Castro, and reinstall a democratic government.

This operation launched in 1961, attacking at a place known as the Bay of Pigs, but the mission was a complete disaster. Most of the invasion was wiped out. Sending soldiers into Cuba caused a pretty big diplomatic problem between the United States and the USSR, and all that came to a head in an epic showdown one year later.

In 1962, the Soviet Union transported nuclear missiles to Cuba and pointed them all at the United States.

American reconnaissance airplanes discovered the nukes, and JFK had a tough call to make—stand up to Moscow and risk a nuclear showdown or back down and let the Soviets build missile bases in Cuba.

He decided to be tough. He sent American warships to blockade Cuba, intercept any Soviet ships, and send them back to the USSR.

It was a hard-core poker move. For thirteen days, JFK and Soviet premier Nikita Khrushchev went eyeball-to-eyeball, with the fate of the world hanging in the balance.

The world sighed with relief when the Soviets finally backed down and agreed to remove the warheads from Cuba. JFK, for his part, took American nukes out of Turkey (which was close to the USSR), and disaster was averted. To this day, it is probably the closest the world has ever come to a full-on nuclear war.

Another problem JFK faced during his presidency was a conflict taking place in Vietnam. After a Communist uprising in northern Vietnam had overthrown the French colonial government, the country was embroiled in a civil war. JFK sent American Green Berets and CIA operatives to South Vietnam to train soldiers and help counter the Communists, but it quickly became clear that the South Vietnamese were going to have a really tough time holding back the Communist forces. This would be the beginning of the bloodiest war in modern American history, and it all got started under JFK.

On November 22, 1963, JFK was assassinated while driving in a motorcade through Dallas, Texas. There are about a billion conspiracy theories about this murder, but the official story here is that JFK was shot by a guy named Lee Harvey Oswald, who was a Communist and was upset about what happened in Cuba.

What the Protest Songs Are About

Kennedy's successor, **Lyndon B. Johnson**, was sworn in as president on an airplane bound for Washington, DC, hours after JFK's death. LBJ had served six terms in the House and two in the Senate, and he went to work immediately trying to battle poverty and further the civil rights efforts Kennedy had begun to put in place. He also continued another JFK project, although this one was a little less wise—he increased the military presence in Vietnam.

Lyndon B. Johnson, thirty-sixth president of the United States

In 1964, LBJ issued a statement that the American warship *Maddox* had come under attack from North Vietnamese torpedo ships in the Gulf of Tonkin, and that this was an act of war that was not going to be tolerated. There's quite a bit of evidence to suggest that maybe things didn't really go down the way LBJ said they did, but the fact remains that America immediately sent a *ton* of soldiers overseas to fight against the Communists in Vietnam.

Tens of thousands of Americans would be killed or wounded in the fighting, and the war would go down as one of the most unpopular conflicts in American history. Riots, public demonstrations, and hundreds of classic rock protest songs would sweep through the United States as the public voiced its discontent with the fighting in Vietnam. Amid all this turmoil, LBJ chose not to run for president in 1968, which paved the way for . . . Richard M. Nixon (and you already know how that went).

The Accidental President

When Nixon and his vice president resigned, the presidency fell to **Gerald**

Ford. Ford's real name was Leslie Lynch King Jr., he was a World War II vet, he'd played football at the University of Michigan, and he was an excellent dancer, but what most people remember about Ford is that one time, in 1975, he  tripped and almost fell over while getting out of a plane. Nowadays he's mostly remembered as a clumsy goober.

Ford was the only president who was never elected as president or vice president (he went from being House minority leader to leader of the Free World in just eight months), and he basically spent most of his presidency trying to get people to forget about Nixon and Watergate. Ford signed another treaty with the Soviet Union to reduce nuclear missiles and signed the Helsinki Accords, which said that America and the

Soviets were going to really, really try to stop threatening to nuke each other every time they had an argument about something.

Ford served the rest of Nixon's second term, but he was not a popular president. In 1974 Ford gave Nixon a full and unconditional pardon for the Watergate incident, a move that upset a lot of people. When Ford ran for reelection in 1976 he lost to Jimmy Carter.

CHAPTER 9
The Modern Presidency

"The real test is not whether you avoid this failure, because you won't. It's whether you let it harden or shame you into inaction, or whether you learn from it."

—Barack Obama

America had the world's first president, and now we see democratically elected presidents and prime ministers on every continent on earth. There is something very admirable about a system of government that tries its hardest to follow the best interests of its population. This is a good thing! But it still isn't perfect.

Jimmy Carter took over for Ford in 1977,

and while he has done some amazing humanitarian work across the globe since his presidency (he won the Nobel Peace Prize in 2002 for his work on human rights), the thing Jimmy Carter is most remembered for as president was an incident known as the Iran Hostage Crisis. In 1979, the leader of Iran was overthrown by an Islamic Revolution, and fifty-two Americans were taken hostage. Carter spent fourteen months trying to get the Americans back, but nothing worked—including sending in counterterrorist Special Forces to try to break them out with a military attack. It took over a year before a release could be negotiated, and by that time so many Americans were angry about this that it basically spelled the end of Carter's presidency.

Ronald Reagan took over for Carter, and if you think Trump was the first television personality to be elected president—think again! Reagan was a really famous actor in the old days, probably best known for playing George Gipp in *Knute Rockne, All American,* but he starred in a ton of movies and TV shows in the forties and fifties. Despite his stint in Hollywood, Reagan is best known for his efforts to destroy the Soviet Union once and for all.

In 1980, the Soviets invaded Afghanistan, which is really pretty much always a bad idea. Attacking Afghanistan didn't work well for Alexander the Great, or the British Empire, or the old Russian Empire, and it didn't work out for the Soviet Union, either. Reagan saw an opportunity to give the Soviets their own little version of Vietnam, so the CIA started giving tons of guns, money, missiles, and training to the Afghan people to help them fight back against this invasion. Meanwhile, as the Soviets were stuck in Afghanistan, Reagan started spending *a ton of money* on the military in an effort to outspend the Soviets. Reagan started an arms race in hopes that the Soviet Union would try to keep up and force themselves into bankruptcy. He built aircraft carriers, nuclear submarines, fighter jets, and missile silos. He even threatened to build a space station program called "Star Wars" that was designed to shoot down Soviet nuclear missiles from space.

The Soviet Union was already in a bad economic spot, and this bump in spending put them well over budget. Moderate Soviet premier Mikhail Gorbachev championed programs called *perestroika* and *glasnost*, which tried to make the USSR a more peaceful, democratic environment, but it wasn't enough. The Soviet Union dissolved in 1991, nearly three years after Reagan left office.

George H. W. Bush, Reagan's vice president and former director of the CIA, took over next.

Bush was a WWII hero, he saw the end of the Cold War, and he's probably best known for leading America in the Gulf War, where a coalition of Western and Arab nations worked together to wipe out the entire Iraqi Army in about one hundred hours. Bush also once said "read my lips, no new taxes," and then passed a couple of new taxes, so there's also that.

Bill Clinton came after Bush. Clinton focused primarily on reducing poverty and crime in America, balancing the budget, and achieving the first budget surplus the country had seen in years. He also once temporarily lost the "nuclear football," the armored briefcase that holds all the nuclear launch codes; bombed the heck out of Yugoslavia, Iraq, and Afghanistan; and became the second president ever to be impeached when he was accused of lying under oath when asked about an inappropriate relationship he had with one of his White House interns. Clinton was impeached and put on trial, and it was determined that he hadn't actually done anything illegal after all. None of this hurt his popularity all that much. Clinton would later win two Grammy awards, if you can believe that!

In 2001, **George W. Bush** took over. G. W. was George H. W. Bush's son, marking the second father-son president duo in history. The September 11, 2001, attacks are the main thing that people remember from his presidency.

Bush then tried to finish what his dad started by launching an attack on Iraq to depose its dictator, Saddam Hussein. Bush said that blowing up Hussein was important because Hussein had "weapons of mass destruction," but Hussein did not have weapons of mass destruction—he still got blown up anyway. To keep the peace after the invasion of Iraq in 2003, George W. Bush gave a bunch of weapons, money, and training to Iraqis who opposed Hussein and his regime.

G. W. was succeeded by **Barack Obama**, who became America's first African American president in 2009. Obama created the Affordable Care Act, a national bill that provided health

Barack Obama, the forty-fourth president of the United States

insurance to all Americans; worked to provide more inclusiveness for LGBT citizens; worked to battle climate change; won the 2009 Nobel Peace Prize; and oversaw the capture and defeat of Osama bin Laden, the terrorist leader who had been behind the 9/11 attacks. He ended the fighting in Iraq, but he continued the operation in Afghanistan, which (as of the time of this writing) continues.

Obama gave way to **Donald Trump** at the beginning of 2017. This book is being written early in the Trump administration, so there isn't much to talk about, except that when Trump was elected, he took office with an approval rating of 40 percent, which is among the lowest approval ratings for an incoming president in the history of the United States! We'll just have to wait and see what happens with that, we guess.

Come what may, the US presidency has been one of the foremost institutions of world democracy since George Washington first took the oath in 1789, and it continues to be a beacon of freedom that the world can look up to. Even if sometimes presidents do some pretty dumb things.

They're only people, after all.

TIMELINE

1. **George Washington:** 1789–97
2. **John Adams:** 1797–1801
3. **Thomas Jefferson:** 1801–09
4. **James Madison:** 1809–17
5. **James Monroe:** 1817–25
6. **John Quincy Adams:** 1825–29
7. **Andrew Jackson:** 1829–37
8. **Martin Van Buren:** 1837–41
9. **William Henry Harrison:** 1841
10. **John Tyler:** 1841–45
11. **James K. Polk:** 1845–49
12. **Zachary Taylor:** 1849–50
13. **Millard Fillmore:** 1850–53
14. **Franklin Pierce:** 1853–57
15. **James Buchanan:** 1857–61
16. **Abraham Lincoln:** 1861–65
17. **Andrew Johnson:** 1865–69
18. **Ulysses S. Grant:** 1869–77
19. **Rutherford B. Hayes:** 1877–81
20. **James A. Garfield:** 1881
21. **Chester A. Arthur:** 1881–85
22. **Grover Cleveland:** 1885–89
23. **Benjamin Harrison:** 1889–93
24. **Grover Cleveland:** 1893–97
25. **William McKinley:** 1897–1901
26. **Theodore Roosevelt:** 1901–09
27. **William Howard Taft:** 1909–13
28. **Woodrow Wilson:** 1913–21
29. **Warren G. Harding:** 1921–23
30. **Calvin Coolidge:** 1923–29
31. **Herbert Hoover:** 1929–33
32. **Franklin D. Roosevelt:** 1933–45
33. **Harry S. Truman:** 1945–53
34. **Dwight D. Eisenhower:** 1953–61
35. **John F. Kennedy:** 1961–63
36. **Lyndon B. Johnson:** 1963–69
37. **Richard M. Nixon:** 1969–74
38. **Gerald Ford:** 1974–77
39. **Jimmy Carter:** 1977–81
40. **Ronald Reagan:** 1981–89
41. **George H. W. Bush:** 1989–93
42. **Bill Clinton:** 1993–2001
43. **George W. Bush:** 2001–09
44. **Barack Obama:** 2009–17
45. **Donald Trump:** 2017–?

ACKNOWLEDGMENTS

The authors would like to thank Simon Boughton and Connie Hsu, for believing in this project and giving us the opportunity to write it, and to our agent, Farley Chase of Chase Literary, for helping us work out all the details to make this happen. Thanks also to our editor, Mekisha Telfer, for her excellent work helping us get this book into shape, and Tracy Koontz, for helping us get our facts straight. And, most of all, we would like to thank you, the reader, for taking the time to read this book! Without your support, none of this could be possible. We really hope you liked it.

Erik would like to first thank Ben for the amazing opportunity to work on this project—it really is a dream come true. I, of course, want to acknowledge all my friends and family for their support over the years, as well as any- and everyone who has ever encouraged me to keep on writing.

A very special shout-out to: David Kowalski (for helping to brainstorm the concept of writing about historical failures), Chris Carroll (for introducing me to blogging), Justin Ache (for helping me redesign my website and hosting it), James Lester (for inspiring me to keep the history blog going), Neil Sindicich (for giving me the opportunity to build up my online writing portfolio), Max Michaels (for my first writing gig in print), Damian Fox (for pushing me to pursue publication and helping me put together my first pitch), John Wesley Moody (my college history professor), Jason Whitmarsh (my humanities professor), my Patreon patrons who have financially supported my blogging habit over the years, and to Dani Slader—who put up with me every step of the way.

Finally, I want to thank Meg—for her endless support and love during the craziest year of my life. (If I missed anyone, it's only because I'm already way over my word count.)

Ben would like to thank the lovely and wonderful Thais Melo, for putting up with me while I was trying to get the last of this series completed, and for always being there with kind words, hugs, and support anytime I was feeling overwhelmed by this process. I also want to say thanks to all my friends and family— I know you must have grown tired of hearing presidential facts at some point, so I appreciate that you all still let me drone on and on about them anyway. Thank you also to my boss, Jake, for his patience with my travel schedule for these books, and my coauthor, Erik, for doing some heroic work researching, compiling, organizing, and writing so much of this series . . . I'm really proud of what we've done, and I hope I was able to help do your vision justice. And thank you, as always, to my wonderful agents Farley Chase of Chase Literary and Sean Daily of Hotchkiss, for always having my back no matter how badly my Impostor Syndrome tries to take over.

BIBLIOGRAPHY

Cool Websites

whitehouse.gov/1600/Presidents
history.com/topics/us-presidents
ducksters.com/biography/uspresidents/
usa4kids.com/presidents/Presidents.html
whitehousehistory.org/the-presidents-timeline
ipl.org/div/potus/

Books

Alterman, Eric. *When Presidents Lie*. New York: Penguin Books, 2004.

Bausum, Ann. *Our Country's Presidents*. Washington, DC: National Geographic Partners, 2017.

Boyer, Paul S. *The Oxford Companion to United States History*. Oxford: Oxford University Press, 2001.

Burns, Ken, and Gerald Kelley. *Grover Cleveland, Again!* New York: Knopf Books for Young Readers, 2016.

Chambers, John Whiteclay. *The Oxford Companion to American Military History*. Oxford: Oxford University Press, 1999.

Churchill, Winston. *Heroes of History*. US: Dodd, Mead & Company, Inc., 1968.

Craughwell, Thomas J. *Failures of the Presidents*. Beverly, MA: Fair Winds Press, 2008.

Davis, Kenneth C. *Don't Know Much about the American Presidents*. New York: Hyperion, 2012.

Davis, Todd, and Marc Frey. *The New Big Book of American Presidents*. Philadelphia, PA: RP Classics, 2008.

DeGregorio, William A., and Sandra Lee Stuart. *The Complete Book of U.S. Presidents*. Fort Lee, NJ: Barricade Books, 2009.

Freidel, Frank, and Hugh Sidey. *The Presidents of the United States of America*. Washington, DC: White House Historical Association, 2006.

Genovese, Michael A. *Encyclopedia of the American Presidency*. New York: Facts on File, 2009.

Jacobs, Dale W. *The World Book of America's Presidents*. Chicago, IL: World Book Encyclopedia, Inc., 1982.

Kerrigan, Michael. *Dark History of the American Presidents*. London, UK: Amber Books Ltd, 2011.

Roper, Jon. *The Illustrated Encyclopedia of the Presidents of America*. Wigston, UK: Lorenz Books, 2012.

Tucker, Spencer. *The Encyclopedia of the Cold War*. Santa Barbara, CA: ABC-CLIO, 2007.

INDEX

Numbers in **bold** indicate pages with illustrations

PICTURE CREDITS

Page 7: Library of Congress's Prints and Photographs Division, LC-USZC4-9904; **10:** The Metropolitan Museum of Art, New York, Gift of John Stewart Kennedy, 1897; **21:** Library of Congress, Prints and Photographs Division, LC-DIG-pga-02636; **26:** Library of Congress, Prints and Photographs Division, LC-USZ62-209; **30–31:** Library of Congress, Prints and Photographs Division, LC-USZC2-3796; **34:** *Trail of Tears* by Max Standley courtesy of R. Michelson Galleries; **36:** Library of Congress, Prints and Photographs Division, LC-DIG-ppmsca-36423; **48:** Wikimedia Commons; **52:** Photo by Library Of Congress; **55:** Courtesy of the National Park Service; **59:** Library of Congress, Prints and Photographs Division, LC-DIG-ppmsca-35588; **65:** New York Historical Society, New York, Bequest of Irving S. Olds; **66:** Courtesy of the White House Historical Association (White House Collection); **69:** Library of Congress, Prints and Photographs Division, LC-DIG-pga-04006; **70:** Courtesy of the White House Historical Association (White House Collection); **77:** Courtesy of the White House Historical Association (White House Collection); **83:** Wikimedia Commons; **85:** Library of Congress, Prints and Photographs Division, LC-USZ62-130973; **88:** Courtesy of the U.S. National Archives and Records Administration; **99:** Wikimedia Commons; **103:** 80-G-32640 courtesy of the Naval History & Heritage Command; **108:** courtesy of the U.S. National Archives and Records Administration; **111:** Courtesy of the U.S. National Archives and Records Administration; **121:** Library of Congress, Prints and Photographs Division, LC-USZ62-104961; **124–125:** Photo by Arnold Sachs/Archive Photos; **129:** A755-14a courtesy of the Lyndon Baines Johnson Presidential Library; **139:** Courtesy of the Office of Barack and Michelle Obama.